Mine, Yours, Ours

Burton Albert, Jr.
Pictures by Lois Axeman

Albert Whitman & Company, *Chicago*

Library of Congress Cataloging in Publication Data

Albert, Burton.
    Mine, yours, ours.

    (A Self-starter book)
    SUMMARY: Pictures and brief text illustrate the
concepts of owning and sharing.
    1. Sharing—Juvenile literature. [1. Sharing]
I. Axeman, Lois. II. Title.
BJ1533.G4A4   173   77-9408
ISBN 0-8075-5148-1

Yours.

Ours.

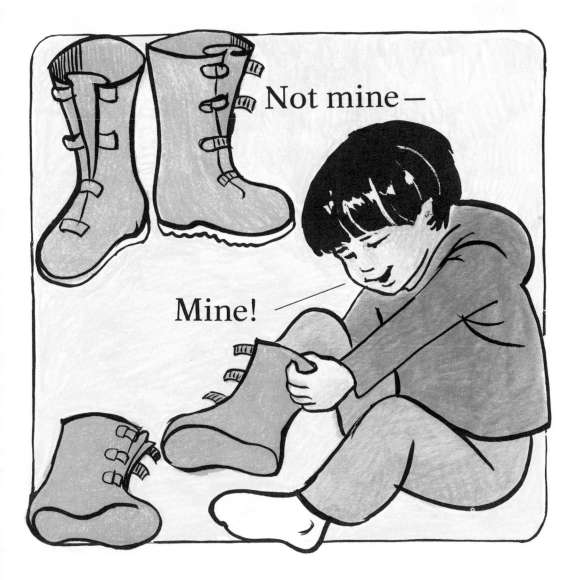

Mine,
yours —
ours.

Is mine—

yours—

and ours?

Yes!

Ours!

My
grandfather.

Our grandfather.

Is
ours—

My friend
is your friend.

Your friends
are
my friends.

My friends, your friends —

OUR friends.

Burton Albert, Jr.

When he isn't in the midst of preparing a new manuscript, Burt Albert might be found photographing old doors and windows, browsing in a bookshop, painting, thumping on the piano, or roaming the shore near his home in Weston, Connecticut. His wife Lois and his daughters Heather and Kelly can be counted on for support in many of these projects.

Mr. Albert has been involved in educational publishing as editor as well as author. He has produced many stimulating school materials to help young people stretch their minds and imaginations as they learn to read and write with enjoyment.

Lois Axeman

Sunshine filters through plants hanging in Lois Axeman's studio windows. More often than not, her small dog Marty, a Shih Tzu, makes himself at home as Mrs. Axeman works on illustrations for a book, a new filmstrip, or art for a textbook.

Courses at the Institute of Design and the American Academy of Art, both in Chicago, prepared Mrs. Axeman for her career. She has illustrated well over twenty books for children and is always ready to experiment with new styles and techniques. Home is a high-rise apartment in Chicago.